Stained Glass Windows

From Philadelphia's Historic
Houses of Worship

by Mary LaCoste
Illustrations by M. Lacoste

Zeta Publishing
Ocala, FL

Copyright © 1989, 2017 by Mary LaCoste

All rights reserved. No part of this publication may be reproduced, distributed, or transmitted in any form or by any means, including photocopying, recording, or other electronic or mechanical methods, without the prior written permission of the publisher, except in the case of brief quotations embodied in critical reviews and certain other noncommercial uses permitted by copyright law. For permission requests, write to the publisher, addressed "Attention: Permissions Coordinator," at the address below.

Zeta Publishing, Inc
3850 SE 58th Ave
Ocala, FL 34480
www.zetapublishing.com

Permission to copy will be granted teachers for classroom use.

Ordering Information:
Quantity sales. Special discounts are available on quantity purchases by corporations, associations, and others. For details, contact the publisher at the address above.
Orders by U.S. trade bookstores and wholesalers. Please contact Zeta Publishing: Tel: (352) 694-2553; Fax: (352) 694-1791 or visit www.zetapublishing.com

First Published by LaCoste in 1989

Rev. Date: Nov. 2nd, 2017

ISBN: 978-1-947191-52-5 (sc)

ISBN: 978-1-947191-53-2 (e)

Library of Congress Control Number: 2017959452

Printed in the United States of America

INDEX

Glorida Dei Church "Old Swedes."..6
St. Peter's Church...10
Old Pine Street Church..14
St. Joseph's Church..18
Mother Bethiel A.M.E. Church...22
Congregation Bnai Abraham and Mikveh Israel Cemetery..27

Walking Tour and Map..28

Christ Church...30
Mikveh Israel and Old First Reformed Church..34
Old St. Augustine's Catholic Church..38
Historic St. George's Church..42
Friend's Meeting House...47

Instructions for Working with the Designs..48
Stained Glass Technology..49
Window Watching..50
Photographing Stained Glass..51
Glass and Spirit..52
Center City Churches Have Heart..54

INTRODUCTION

Religious freedom was of such great importance to William Penn that when he established his colony of Pennsylvania and planned the "city of brotherly love", Philadelphia, he welcomed persons of many religious denominations as settlers. As a Quaker, Penn had himself felt the sting of religious persecution in England. The charter of his new colony contained words guaranteeing a measure of religious tolerance. As a result, people of many faiths flocked to his land which came to be called "the holy experiment". Years later these ideals would be echoed in the constitution of the United States, written in Philadelphia.

Today, a legacy of William Penn remains in the unusual number of historically important churches to be found in the heart of his old city. Some are the founding churches of their denomination in America. In this book are included several of importance that are in walking distance of one another. While their histories and present activities are summarized, the spotlight is on their windows, many of which are outstanding examples of American stained glass making artistry from the golden age of stained glass in this country - 1870 to 1900.

Of these windows, few have received notice from anyone outside of their congregations and some are even hidden from them in church basements and storage areas. In most cases the artists and craftsmen have been forgotten.

It is hoped that this book will bring the light of attention to these inspiring, shimmering works of art, these hidden treasures from the past still able to illuminate minds and hearts today.

Gloria Dei Church "Old Swedes"

Columbus Blvd. & Christian St.

Sunday Services, 10 AM
www.info@oldswedes.org

Charming Gloria Dei Church, the oldest house of worship in the Delaware valley, is often the site of weddings. It was founded by Swedish Lutheran settlers before the area became an English colony. The first Church building was made of logs and was replaced by the present building in 1698.

Today the church overlooks the Delaware river and the i-95 highway. It is surrounded by a historic cemetery that includes a monument to the first president of our country, a man of Swedish ancestry named John Hanson.*

In the middle of the last century, the congregation voted to change its affiliation to the Episcopal Church. Near that time, the church was renovated but retained its colonial design. The pulpit was moved to the east end of the church in front of a large window. This probably led to the installation of the stained-glass panel as bright sun coming through that window would have made it difficult for the congregation to see the minister. Today a venetian blind adds further light control.

The Church, often called "Old Swedes' church", now has a small but active congregation. Late each fall it sponsors the Saint Lucia festival when many Swedish folk customs are recalled.

Gloria Dei is a most interesting place to visit. It is a mile and a half south of the historic park, is easily reached by public transportation and has ample parking. There is a gift shop with limited hours that sells items relating to the religious and cultural significance of the Church.

---

*Mr. Hanson was president of the Continental Congress, Washington was the first president elected by the public.

These four stained glass panels from the Gloria Dei Church have a bright red border with simple vines and flowers that resemble Swedish folk art, perhaps as a reminder of Gloria Dei's origins. The shields have blue edges and white backgrounds, one with a red cross and the other with a silver dove. These designs are typical of Episcopal Church tradition. Around the shield is silvery grey glass with red diagonal lines crossing beneath the shield and again above it. The crossing point under the shield is a blue diamond shape. A little further out there is an open diamond shape of blue behind the red lines. The effect is almost like plaid and may echo an earlier lattice shutter at the window. Today, the sun shinning through the glass casts a cross shaped shadow formed by the wood between the window sections.

At the top of the stained glass window are the pictures of two angels that remind the viewer of the two carved cherubim hanging in the rear of the church. This carving is older than the church building itself and dates from the earliest Swedish colonial days.

St. Peter's Church

Philadelphia, PA 19106
313 Pine Street

info@stpetersphilla.org
Sunday Services, 9 & 11 AM
Phone number: 215-924-5968

St. Peter's Episcopal Church today looks very much as it did when it first opened in 1761 except for the tall steeple added a century later. Inside, the brick flooring is still as it was in colonial times and the high-backed box pews are the original ones. An unusual feature is the placement of the wooden pulpit at the opposite end of the church from the altar.

In the churchyard that surrounds St. Peter's are a row of Osage orange trees that were sent as seedlings from the Lewis and Clark expedition, the first trees of this type to be seen east of the Mississippi river. Nearby, the tombstones of many famous people are to be found. Unmarked are the graves of several Indian chiefs who died of yellow fever while on a peace mission to Philadelphia in the 1790's.

An active parish today, St. Peter's serves the needs of a varied congregation. The private school next to the church was founded by the parish.

Audio tours available.

St. Paul's Church
Third street at willings alley

St. Paul's Church also opened its doors in 1761. It closed in 1901 and it's parishioners joined the congregation at nearby St. Peters. The building was used for many years as a city mission and now houses the offices of the Episcopal Community Services. Saved from it's days as a mission is a stained glass panel with a large red heart that once hung over the main door. It is shown on the last page of this book and can possibly be found stored in an Episcopal services office.

The stained glass windows of St. Peter's Church were made by the royal Bavarian glass company of Munich and New York and were probably added near the turn of the century. They depict scenes from the life of Christ and were mounted on the inner sides of the major windows. At a later time it was felt that they were not appropriate for a colonial Georgian style church so they were removed from the side windows. Two stained glass windows remain in the tower & three behind the altar. The center one is shown here.

The Jesus figure is clothed in red with a white over-garment. The children and other figures are wearing a variety of colors. There is a vivid blue sky and green and tan grass. The wood pieces dividing the panels are white. The colors are jewel toned and are particularly lovely when the morning sun shines through them.

Old Pine Street Church

412 Pine Street
Philadelphia, PA 19106

Phone number: 215-925-8051
info@oldpine.org
Sunday Services, 10:30 AM

The Third, Scots and Mariners Presbyterian Church is more often called by the informal name, "the Old Pine Street Church". The reverend Mr Duffield was perhaps the congregation's most famed pastor. His sermons were heard by George Washington and John Adams. He became one of the chaplains of the Continental Congress and joined Washington's army as did over 60 of the men from Old Pine Street Church. When the British occupied Philadelphia, the soldiers used the church as a hospital, burned the pews for firewood, and eventually turned the church into a stable.

The church building once looked very much like Saint Peter's Church which is one block away. The brick colonial style was changed in the last century to a classical style with large Greek columns and a covering of light yellow stucco and the floor was raised to create space for a ground level Sunday school.

Stained glass windows with geometric designs were added in the 1880's. A few years later, two sets of lovely windows with curving lines and flowers were installed and are pictured here.

The Old Pine Street Church is surrounded by an interesting and historic cemetery. Almost all of the city block is owned by the Presbyterian Church. Next to the cemetery is a community center and alongside it is the Presbyterian historical society building.

Old pine is still an active parish with members from all walks of life. It sponsors musical and other cultural events, social services and provides direct aid to homeless persons.

Called "art nouveau" windows, these lovely panels from the Old Pine Church may be of a type that was a forerunner of that style. They are symmetrical and feature curving lines of stylized vines, flowers and classical motifs. A variety of colors and glass textures were used, the round pieces giving a jewel like effect.

The design with the arched top is not only symmetrical but the top half is almost a mirror image of the bottom. The sample from the rectangular window features an elaborate shell design and could be called embellished classical or renascence design. These windows are among the best examples of American decorative glass to be found anywhere.

The square window has a yellow border edged in orange with light blue jewels. Every color but purple appears in the rest of the panel and in the arched window. The dominating colors are earth tones. In actuality, the color values appear to change with the time of day and the season.

St. Joseph's Church

321 Willings Alley
Philadelphia, PA 19106

Phone number: 215-923-1733
www.oldstjosephs.org
Masses:
Sundays, 6:30 PM
Weekdays, 12:05 PM
Saturdays, 6:30 PM

"When in 1733 St. Joseph's Roman Catholic Church was founded ... It was the only place in the entire English speaking world where public celebration of the...Mass was permitted by law."

.....these words are found on a bronze plaque on the wall of St. Joseph's, Philadelphia's oldest Catholic Church.

Built without a steeple and located in the middle of a city block, the first Saint Joseph's Church was designed to be inconspicuous. Although William Penn was determined that there be religious freedom in his new colony, English law forbade public Catholic worship and mass was not officially tolerated until 1734.

The present church is the third to be built on the site but still has no steeple and is hard to find. It can be reached by way of an alley from Fourth Street or from Walnut Street by walking through a small park that replaced buildings that once hid that side from view.

Saint Joseph's University had its beginnings at old Saint Joseph's Church as did many other educational and religious organizations. Staffed by the Jesuit fathers, Saint Joseph's is a parish church, provides noontime liturgical services for downtown office workers and participates in programs to feed homeless people.

St. Mary's, one block away, was built in 1763 to accommodate the growing Catholic population. It is said that George Washington visited it and attended services. The church has been renovated several times and is an interesting mix of styles. The stained glass is of the traditional pictorial variety, much of it of European origin. Above the altar is a huge expanse of stained glass illuminated by a smaller window several feet behind it. It portrays a crucifixion scene and is believed to be from Insbruck. It does, however, have a Philadelphia signature. No attempt has been made to replicate the window here because of its complexity.

There are no records of the identity of the craftsmen who installed the stained glass windows in Saint Joseph's Church. Very probably they were done in the decade before the turn of the century. Some of the windows are of a traditional religious pictorial style while others are abstract designs with brightly colored swirls and intricately stylized decorations.

Shown here is a medallion section picturing St. Joseph. The lilies are a conventional means of identifying him as Joseph and recall a traditional story about his life. The background is blue and the garments are brown and blue.

The abstract windows are predominately yellow and orange with touches of light blue and green and have a narrow band of red around the sides. Eight of the side windows are like the tall one shown here. The design continues upward to matching balcony windows and combine to produce, on a sunny day, a marvelous golden glow in the church.

The other abstract window is high on the wall near the sanctuary. It has been blocked by a building addition and receives no exterior light. As a result, this window appears to be a curious brown door.

Mother Bethel A. M. E. Church

419 Richard Allen Avenue
Philadelphia, PA 19147
Phone number: 215-925-0616
info@motherbethel.com
Services, Sundays at 9:30 AM

Mother Bethel
African Methodist Episcopal Church
founded on this site 1787
By
Richard Allen
(A former slave)

This ground, purchased by Richard Allen for a Church, is the oldest parcel of real estate owned continuously by Negroes in the United States. This congregation is the world's oldest African Methodist Episcopal Church congregation.

These words are found on a bronze plaque on the front of the present Mother Bethel A. M. E. Church, the fourth to occupy the site. It is a large stone edifice constructed in the Romanesque style in 1889.

Richard Allen was, at one time, a preacher for St. George's Methodist Church but left there in 1787 with a number of his followers because of racial discrimination. Leaving with him was Absalom Jones who later became an Episcopal priest and founded St. Thomas's Episcopal Church. In 1793 these two leaders distinguished themselves by their help with victims of the yellow fever plague.

Francis Asbury, "the Father of American Methodism", who had been sent from England by John Wesley, ordained the Rev. Allen and dedicated his Church. In 1797, however, the African Methodist Episcopal Church incorporated entirely apart from the old congregation. Richard Allen became bishop of the new church which has been mother church to hosts of other A.M.E. congregations over the years.

The stained glass windows in the present church building are truly remarkable examples of the glass made in America in the late nineteenth century. The curves of the structure are echoed throughout the patterns in the windows and are executed in brilliant and opalescent glass with a harmonious interplay of colors. Designs with symbolic meaning appear as do biblical cities and a large figure of Christ. Recently, the Richard Allen window was designed and installed conforming to the older designs. It is shown on the title page of this book. The window opposite is on the cover.

Congregation Bnai Abraham

521 Lombard St.
Philadelphia, PA 19147
Phone number: 215-238-2100
www.phillyshul.com

The B'nai Abraham congregation was founded in 1890 by a group of Othodox Jewish families who emigrated from Russia and Lithuania over one hundred years ago. The synagogue, built in 1891, still serves descendants of the original worshipers. The congregation was quite large at one time but is now small as many of the families have moved from center city. On major holidays, however, many members of the old flock return.

The synagogue looks quite contemporary but it's design is little changed from the year it was built. The sanctuary is illuminated by a series of lovely opalescent side windows in with stylized designs framing panels picturing seven branched candlesticks. Over the entrance is a large wheel window with the Star of David at the hub.

B'nai Abraham Synagogue is located on Lombard Street around the corner from Mother Bethel and separated from it only by a corner parking lot. Because the windows are made of opalescent glass, their design can easily be seen from the outside. For full color effect, however, they should be seen from the interior where the sections that seemed soft green on the outside turn to a magnificent glowing yellow-gold.

Mikveh Israel Cemetary

800 block of Spruce St.

Long before the first synagogue was built in Philadelphia, a cemetery for the use of the Jewish community was established on land purchased from William Penn by Nathan Levi, a merchant whose ship, it is said, brought the Liberty Bell to America.

Among the famous Americans buried there are Haym Salomon, who is known as the financier of the revolution, and several Jewish revolutionary war soldiers. The cemetery can be viewed through large wrought iron gates installed in 1802.

Map for walking tours

All but the first of the houses of worship mentioned in this book are in walking distance of one another. As you may want to see the stained glass windows in their settings, I have suggested two rather pleasant routes and numbered the stops. One covers the churches south of chesnut street which are discussed in the first half of the book. The others, numbered 7 to 12, are north of Chestnut.

The oldest house of worship in Philadelphia is Gloria Dei. For that reason I listed it first. Since that would be quite a hike, you may want to call SEPTA. For directions to a convenient bus at 215-580-7800. Don't bypass this remarkable church and cemetery, now supervised by the National Park Service. However, you may want to reschedule it at different time. It does have ample parking.

Philadelphia has many broad landscaped paths through the centers of urban blocks. Several are indicated on the map by dotted lines. The stroll from St. Peter's to St. Joseph's Church by way of Delaney Park is particularly nice.

While you are in the area you may want to view the Mikvah Israel Cemetery before calling it a day or heading for the next part of the walk.

The second walk begins at Christ Church. Remember that the stained glass there is stored but the Palladian window and other features are interesting. While seeing Mikva Israel Synagogue, you may want to visit the national museum of American Jewish history. Exit by the 5th street side that takes you though a garden with benches. Go north and turn onto arch where you will see the Christ Church cemetery.

After the Old Reformed Church you will see the Ben Franklin bridge. You will pass under it for the next two stops. Then you will walk south to the Friends Meeting House. On the northern walk you will notice that there is no lack of places to eat or shop!

Many of the houses of worship are routinely open from 10 until 4 pm. Telephone ahead if you wish to be sure to get inside a particular one.

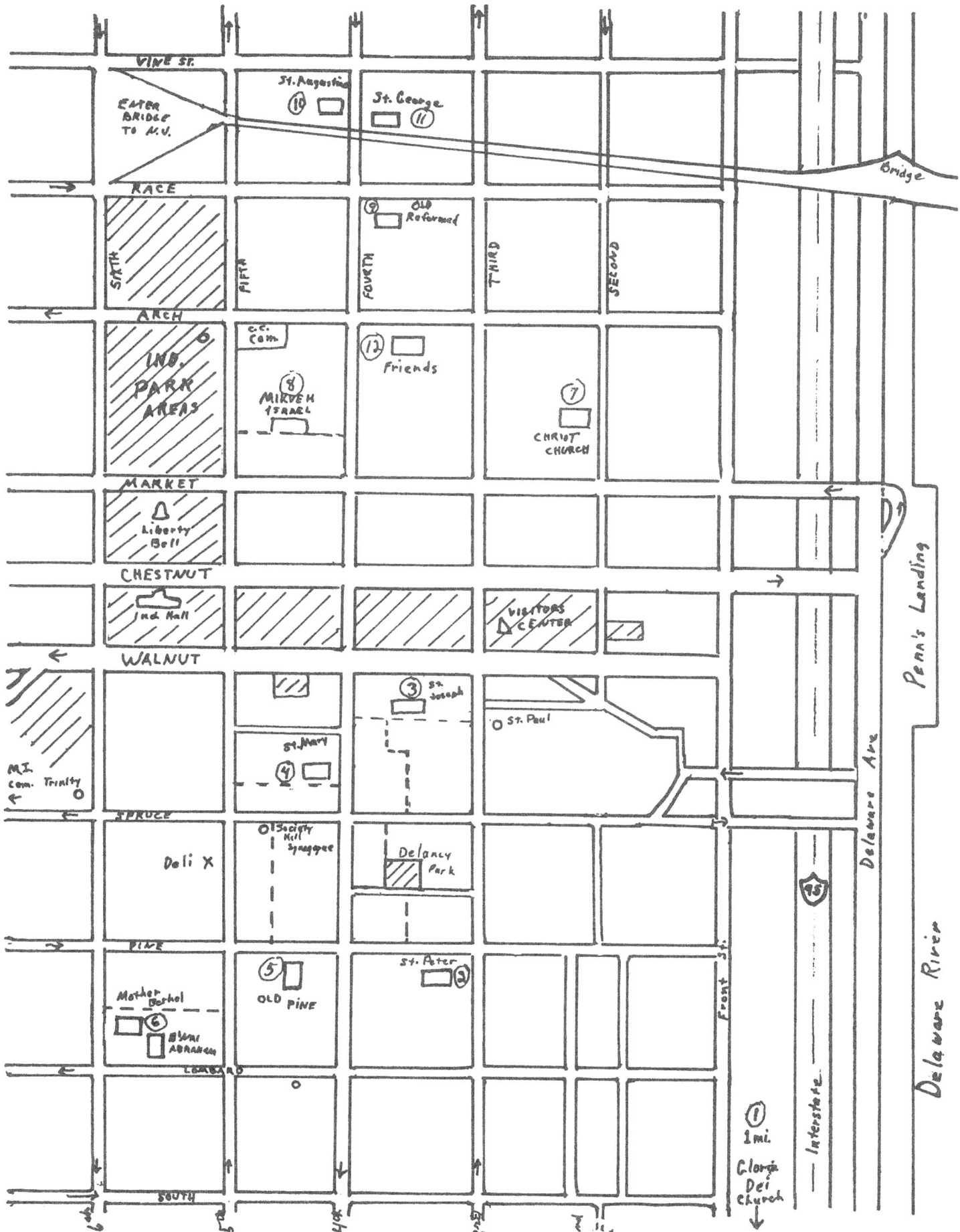

Christ Church

20 Second Street
Philadelphia, PA 19106
Phone number: 215-922-1695
www.christChurchphila.org

Sunday Services:
10:10 AM

Christ Church was founded in 1695 and was the only Church of England parish in Philadelphia for over half a century. The first Church building was replaced by the present impressive structure in 1727. It is of Georgian style with lovely Palladian windows. Years after it was built, Ben Franklin helped with the design of the steeple.

After the Revolutionary War, American Anglicans wanted to be independent of the Church of England. There were no bishops in the newly formed United States. Dr. William White, pastor of Christ Church and former chaplain of the continental congress, was selected to become the first bishop of the diocese of Pennsylvania. He had to travel to great Britain for consecration despite the risk of being considered an enemy by that country. At Christ Church, the Episcopal Church of the United States was formed in 1789.

Christ Church is the most frequently visited of all of Philadelphia's historic churches and is a short stroll from the liberty bell and other independence area attractions. It remains, however, an active parish serving the needs of a congregation.

There is a small churchyard surrounding Christ Church which serves as a pleasant place for city people to sit. The main burial ground is two blocks west where the graves of Ben Franklin and many other persons prominent in American history can be found.

The congregation of Christ Church is proud of the fact that many famous Americans have worshiped in their historic church. In the early part of this century they contracted with an English firm to make the stained glass shown here. It pictures prominent revolutionary figures seated in the church. It was installed in the left front window and named "the patriot's window".

In recent years, it was decided to restore the interior of Christ Church to the decor of the time of the Declaration of Independence. Since stained glass was not in use in the colonies at that time, all of the stained glass, including the patriot's window, were removed and stored. It is hoped that one day funds will be found to display the windows once more, perhaps in the church house.

Congregation Mikveh Israel

44 North Fourth Street
Phildelphia, PA 19106
Phone number: 215-922-5446
info@MikvehIsrael.org
Services Friday at sunset and 9 AM on Saturday

Mikveh Israel first built a synagogue in 1782 on Third and Cherry streets not far from the present location. In 1976, after many years away from the Independence Hall area, Mikveh Israel moved into a beautifully designed new synagogue built in conjunction with the museum of American Jewish history. The interior of the building is traditionally furnished in the manner of the Spanish-Portuguese orthodox Jewish ritual.

Separate from the Synagogue but nearby, the national museum of Jewish history is open to the public. It features permanent and changing exhibits relating to religious history and to the contributions of Jewish culture to American life. There is also a gift shop with many items of interest including hand crafted menorahs like the stained glass one pictured here. For more information call 215-923-3811. www.nmajh.org

Old First Reformed Church

United Church of Christ
151 N. 4th St.
Philadelphia, PA 19106
215-922-4566
admin@oldfirstucc.org
Services 10 AM Sundays

Established in 1727, old First Reformed Church is one of the oldest reformed congregations in America. Their first house of worship was a small six sided church which was replaced with a larger structure just prior to the Revolutionary War. In 1882 the church members decided to move to another part of the city and sold their building to a paint company.

When Philadelphia began renewal efforts in the 1960's, the congregation learned that their former church building was for sale. They bought and painstakingly restored it.

Today the church looks much as it did long ago. It is not considered a museum but is a very active parish serving people from the neighborhood and from the suburbs. Among the church's various programs is one providing food and housing for homeless men.

Displayed in the church office are four "plates" depicting each of the former church buildings. It has been discovered recently that they are, in fact, center medallions from leaded glass windows. The one shown here is of the very first church. There is a bird rather than a cross on top, an old German tradition.

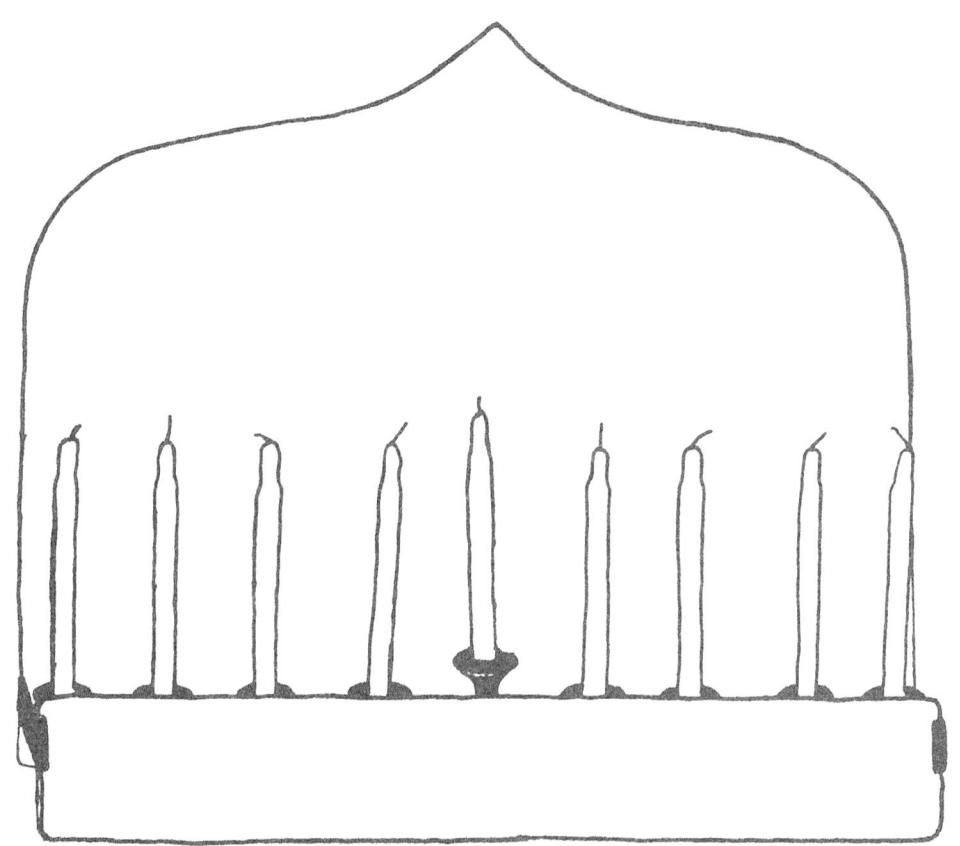

The Lamp

The Hannukkah lamp shown here was found in the gift shop of the museum of Jewish history. It is made of medium blue stained glass held together by black metal. The glass has a slightly textured finish with wispy streaks.

Diagonal stripes in pastel colors will give the candles a spiraled look. If you want to add flames to the wicks, leave a round space uncolored at the candle tips. The fire can be drawn on the front of the picture or hidden on the back where it can be seen when the paper is held up to light.

The Plate

The round plate is from a display case at the First Reformed Church. It is twelve inches across and is surrounded by grooved lead that once held it in place in a window. The glass has an etched finish.

Old St. Augustine's Catholic Church

243 N. Lawrence St.
Philadelphia, PA 19106

Phone number: 215-627-1838
www.st-augustineChurch.com
Services Saturday at 5:15
Sunday 9 & 11 AM & 7 PM

George Washington contributed funds for the building of St. Augustine's Church in 1796. Unlike St. Joseph's Catholic Church some sixty years earlier, it was not a hidden house of worship but enjoyed the religious freedom and more tolerant public attitude of the new nation.

By the 1840s however, strong anti-catholic feelings grew fueled by the competition for jobs occasioned by the massive numbers of immigrants from Ireland and Germany. In 1844 there was a riot in which St. Augustine's Church, library and school were burned to the ground. It is said that the rioters would have torched other religious structures were it not for the action of a group of Quakers who formed a line and bravely asked the rioting mob to refrain from crossing it.

The general public was shocked by the riot and many groups helped with recovery including the leaders of the Methodist Church across the street. Eventually some funds were awarded to the parish through court action.

The second St. Augustine's Church was dedicated in 1847 and stands today. The style is called Palladian-Baroque, a term also used to describe Christ Church built a century earlier. The parish has long been served by Augustine Friars.

The stained glass in the side windows of St. Augustine's Church is highly decorative and embellished but has classical lines that harmonize with the Church exterior. The window shown here with the lamb symbol is predominantly light yellow with blue ribbons and swags of colorful fruit at the top. The border has red, blue and gold designs.

In the stair area there are two tall windows with much simpler lines and a stark geometric style. Much of the glass is cloudy white with a border of alternating pink and blue squares with an inner border of blue. The sun design is made of two narrow bands of yellow with blue triangles around it. Small circles of blue glass, called roundels, complete the top pattern. The band under it has yellow roundels set in green with yellow borders. Other color combinations would work well. This is a good window to use for trying creative ideas.

Historic St. George's Church

235 North Fourth Street
Philadelphia, PA 19106
215-925-7788
www.historicstgeorges.org

Sunday Service at 11 AM

Open to visitors Tuesdays through Fridays
From 10 AM to 4 PM

Old St. George's Church is the world's oldest Methodist Church in continuous service and is considered the cradle of American Methodism. The building was named and built by a denomination that ran out of funds as it neared completion. In 1769, a Methodist group founded two years earlier was able to purchase it at a bargain price. It seemed an answer to a prayer as the young congregation urgently needed a larger church.

For many years St. George's was the home base for Francis Asbury who is called "the father of the Methodist Church in America". Sent from England by John Wesley, the reverend Asbury traveled over a quarter of a million miles on horseback in a period of 45 years to preach his gospel message.

Attached to St. George's is a museum with many mementos important to American history and the story of the growth of Methodism. Of particular interest are the pieces of equipment used by the fearless circuit riders.

Attempts were made to demolish this historic landmark as it was in the path of approaches to the Ben Franklin bridge. There was such an outcry of protest that plans were changed and the church now lies in the shadow of the bridge.

The interior of the church is colonial style with balconies and a chandelier that supports tall candles. The white painted pews and walls combine with large clear glass windows to give it a lovely light atmosphere. At the turn of the century, the street side of the church had leaded windows with stained glass trim. They are now stored in the church's sub-basement.

Pictured here, the windows are an example of a restrained nec-classical style and are made to open and close. They have a ribbon of green ending in a stylized leaf and palm design. The edges are a deep orange and the large center parts are a translucent silvery grey. The four round pieces are almost white.

FRIENDS MEETING HOUSE

Fourth and Arch Streets
Philadelphia, PA 19106
Services on Sundays at 10 AM

Open to visitors 10 Am to
4 PM daily except Sunday
215-413-1804
www.archstreetfriends.org

William Penn established the colony of Pennsylvania in 1682. He was a "Quaker" which means that he belonged to the religious society of friends. He felt strongly that there should be religious tolerance in his new colony so he welcomed and encouraged settlers of all faiths as well as his own. The fact that today there are so many historic houses of worship in Philadelphia is a legacy he left to his "city of brotherly love".

The historic Friends Meeting House at Fourth and Arch Street was built in 1804 and furnished in part with items from previous meeting houses. In keeping with the Quaker philosophy of plainness and simplicity, the building is well made but unadorned. To the casual observer, the exterior looks almost contemporary. Inside, centuries old benches are still to be found but modern objects are used where they are needed. An example is the venetian blind used to control glare.

Services are still held in the building twice a week and it is open for visitors every day but Sunday. The members of the society no longer wear plain clothing or use "thee" and "thou" in everyday conversation, but they retain a dedication to the promotion of peace and brotherhood.

The window shown here is located on the north side of the large meeting hall and overlooks a walled yard with typical Philadelphia houses beyond. As much of the glass is original, it gives a slightly wavy appearance. A Quaker Meeting House would never use stained glass, but this window with the view of the tree may be just as colorful in the fall when the leaves are changing as any stained glass. In the spring when the tree is in bloom it may be even more inspiring of prayerful thought.

INSTRUCTIONS FOR WORKING WITH DESIGNS

Note that all stained glass designs are positioned in the book in such a way that no text appears on the back. You can detach and mount your finished work to a window or other light source to get a translucent effect.

Water color is one of the most realistic ways to simulate stained glass color. Let a section dry before painting in neighboring colors to minimize bleeding. Going over the lead lines with a sharpened wax crayon will also help prevent bleeding.

Crayons are easy to use but care must be taken to get full coverage. Rubbing colored sections with tissues helps.

Color sticks* are a new product that look like long crayons but are erasable!

Colored pencils have the advantage of fine points for intricate designs. The results can be made more vivid by wetting the paper slightly either before of after applying color.

Felt Markers are vivid but should be used with care. Test the shades and line widths on scrap paper. Be cautious with yellow markers as they pick up darker colors and then produce muddy lines. It helps to color the yellow sections first.

Combining media can produce pleasant results. Emphasis, shading and special effects can be achieved by coloring on the back side of the paper. Experiment on scrap paper or photocopy the designs to make practice sheets.

Experiment! Photocopy the designs to try different techniques. You can even try translucent paper. The backs of pages can be used to add shading, combine colors or for special effects. They will show through when the designs are mounted in a window or light source.

---

*copyright, Crayola product, Binney & Smith

STAINED GLASS TECHNOLOGY

The term "stained glass" is used to describe many types of colored glass used in windows. The glass can be thick or thin, smooth, bumpy or patterned and can have various degrees of translucency and reflect-ability. The basic color comes from minerals added to the glass in its molten state. Other coloring materials can be fused to the surface of the glass by baking. This is how detail lines and shadings are added.

After a design is made, glass pieces are selected and cut to fit the desired pattern. The pieces are held in place with strips of lead soldered together. Sections are mounted in a frame and strengthened with metal reinforcing rods. Once in a window opening, a piece of clear glass or plastic can be installed on the outside for added protection. In very modern designs, an artist sometimes chooses to use chunks of vividly colored glass set in cement or epoxy and avoids the use of lead supports.

When a religious body wants to commission a stained glass window, a committee can be formed to meet with an artist or a stained glass making company. The ideas the congregation wants to express and ways to do it are discussed. The artist draws designs for approval. When they agree, the designs are turned over to craftsmen who make the windows and install them. Often, after a period of time, the names of the artist and the craftsmen are forgotten. Unfortunately only a few stained glass windows are signed.

The most famous American stained glass designer was Louis Comfort Tiffany, but even some of his works remain unidentified. He and John Lefarge developed a type of material known as opalescent glass. It has a lovely luminous quality and was widely used in the years near the turn of the century. Many opalescent windows can be found in churches today. They can easily be spotted by the fact that the design and some of the colors can be seen in daylight on the outside of the church, not just from inside. This is because the minerals in the glass cause it to reflect back part of the light instead of letting it all pass through. As a result these windows do not light up the church interior quite as well as windows with traditional glass but with artificial lighting this is not a problem.

Over the years there have been controversies about what kinds of glass and what styles and designs are best for houses of worship. One school of thought holds that only the most transparent and vibrantly colored glasses should be used and that shadings and added lines should be kept to a minimum. Others think that the windows should be made to look like ones in ancient European cathedrals, even if this means adding artificial aging. A contemporary view would avoid pre-set rules and focus on total effect.

WINDOW WATCHING

"Window watching" can grow into a fascinating pastime leading to new understanding of architectural styles, social trends and religious thought. Starting with your own house of worship and neighboring religious structures, you will find yourself wanting answers to questions about the designers of the stained glass, the meanings of the symbols and the eras in which they were installed. Pieces of information you already possess will be linked together to form new more complex ideas, not unlike the ways the pieces of glass work together to make lucid pictures.

Some questions this book may bring to mind are:

> Why do the windows pictured here have arched or square tops instead of pointed ones?
>
> Why weren't stained glass windows put in the colonial churches when they were first built?
>
> Are there names for the kinds of designs?

Some answers may be found in the history of stained glass making, a craft that had its beginnings in America in the 1800s. The Victorian era with its need for decorative glass inspired great production in the United States after 1850. In the same period large amounts of traditional pictorial glass was imported from England and Germany. By the "golden age" of American stained glass, 1880 to 1910, every large American city had stained glass studios and Philadelphia developed some of the best. Stained glass was of good quality, inexpensive and readily available. Almost all congregations wanted these colorful windows for their old or new churches.

The Victorian era was a time of revivals of many older building traditions, particularly the grand Gothic style with tall pointed arches and glorious windows. Some church men felt that as Gothic was the only architectural style developed by Christian culture it was more appropriate for church buildings than Roman or Greek styles that had their origins in pagan civilizations. Others maintained that Gothic style was much too "popish" for protestant churches. As theology was more important than style to religious groups, decoration was often mixed and Gothic windows would be put in colonial churches and abstract in those of classical design. The results are often charming rather than incongruous.

PHOTOGRAPHING STAINED GLASS

Taking pictures of stained glass is not difficult. Windows don't move so you can take your time. A particularly nice photo can be made into a personalized holiday card.

You do not have to have a sunny day to photograph windows, a slightly overcast day will do well and may produce richer tones. Check your camera instruction book for adjusting to light conditions.

While sunny days do produce good pictures, avoid having the sun shining through at such an angle that the sun "spot" is in your viewer. This will produce a "hot" area in your picture.

Try to take the pictures in natural light whenever possible. Use the flash when you want to study the lead lines and design as this will all but eliminate the colors. (I did this to study the lines for this book.) Exceptions are opalescent windows which sometimes look better with flash.

To really understand a window, examine it closely, look for signatures (rare), take it with flash and without and also from outside. Try different angles. Usually the best pictures are taken in line with the center of the design. As church windows are usually high above your head, there will be some distortion. Get as high as you can or use a telephoto lens.

Focusing on a detail of a design can produce good pictures, particularly if you take a series of details relating to one theme. I know someone who "collects" angels from stained glass.

You will notice that the colors in the glass will vary with the season, the time of day and the weather. It is fun to catch these subtle differences in photographs.

Glass and the Spirit

In the middle ages when ordinary persons could not read or write, stained glass was used as a means of instructing the faithful. The windows could be seen by many people at one time and served as large religious picture books. Even abstract ideas were communicated by the use of symbols. Although illiteracy is no longer common stained glass can still have a teaching function.

Television has made people more visually aware today and has accustomed them to seeing pictures dance before their eyes to convey messages. Stained glass images do not move or make sounds. A person's intellect must interact with the frozen designs to extract meanings. It is possible that beyond the more obvious learnings there may be the added benefit of learning to more actively use one of the mind's less frequently used abilities.

Observing stained glass is pleasurable. The jeweled glass appeals to the eyes and delights them the way music does to the ears. They are part of creating an atmosphere that helps one know that a Church is not part of the everyday world. Even the ordinary sights and sounds are filtered by the glass and distractions are minimized.

These windows can teach, inspire and create an atmosphere leading to thought and contemplation. Yet they may have still another function. They are examples. When no light passes through them they are dark and convey no message. When the sun illuminates them their beauty is shown for all to enjoy. People are like that. They are beauty unrealized until a light illuminates them, and each person must find that light.

CENTER CITY CHURCHES HAVE A HEART

The houses of worship in the historic area of Philadelphia welcome visitors but are not primarily museums. Their main purpose is to serve the spiritual needs of their congregations, a job they seem to do well despite increasing costs of maintaining their facilities with the support of what is often a declining number of members. In addition they try to meet the needs of their communities, many offering services such as day care programs. Often they are the catalyst for neighborhood improvements and cultural events. Some have been named national historic shrines but receive no federal funds for this designation.

Center city Philadelphia has a large number of homeless persons living on its streets. Many of the congregations mentioned here have helped provide them food and some limited shelter. There are soup kitchens in church basements. Clothing and blankets are collected and distributed. Young people from one church walk through the area in the evening distributing soup and sandwiches prepared in the neighboring synagogue. These programs receive support from several congregations and community agencies.

St. Paul's Episcopal Church closed its doors as a parish near the turn of the century. Its members became a part of nearby St. Peter's Church and the building became a mission for the poor. Years later the stained glass panel shown here was placed over the entrance door. Now the building has been completely renovated and houses offices for the Episcopal Community Services.

The Heart Panel was made by Henry Lee Willet of the famed Philadelphia firm, Willet's stained glass studio. When the panel was being made, the heart shaped glass piece bulged up in an irregular fashion when it was fired. Willet decided not to discard the ruby colored glass as the imperfection made the heart look more realistic. At one time the panel was mounted in a box with a light that went on and off like a beating heart! The present location is unknown.

About the Author

This coloring book was first written in 1989, long before adults became interested the delightful hobby of colorizing designs for fun and relaxation. Needless to say, this book did not sell well to grown-ups or to parents of children who found the text too difficult for youngsters. Recently, the folks at Zeta suggested re-issuing it with the updates seen here.

The author, Mary LaCoste, began her interest in stained glass when teaching a religious education class to teenagers in Philadelphia. In the 1990s Mary's husband Al took advantage of an early retirement offer and they returned home to New Orleans, LA. There she wrote a fact book entitled "Death Embraced: New Orleans Tombs and Burial Customs," that is selling well in her native city (and on Amazon too).

Mary is now pursuing a retirement career as a Gray Line tour guide and lecturer in her home town. Still interested in stained glass, she is part of a volunteer group that gives tours of local houses of worship twice a year.

In the past she was a teacher, principal and part time journalist. Now she and Al live in the historic French Quarter of New Orleans to the delight of their many adult grandchildren who love to visit their home. They know it is near historic sites, churches, Mardi Gras parade routes and the music of Bourbon Street.

www.ingramcontent.com/pod-product-compliance
Lightning Source LLC
Chambersburg PA
CBHW081356080526
44588CB00016B/2511